CW00853808

BLESSINGS
FOR THE JOURNEY

ELIZABETH
SHARMAN-SMITH

Author of

JESUS CHRIST A NEVER
ENDING HEALING LOVE

Front Cover Pixel Art
by Elizabeth Sharman-Smith

ISBN: 978-1977978646

For Andrew

I am indebted to Rev Canon Paul Townsend for his Foreword, and for his care and support.

Contents

FOREWORD 1

adoration... 3

belonging... 4

beloved.. 5

blessed.. 6

blessedness 7

blessing 8

blessings... 9

care 10

change 11

changeless.. 12

Christ child... 13

consolation 14

constant 15

dominion 16

empower.. 17

enrichment 18

eternity 19

ever-loving.. 20

everlasting..21

faith 22

faithful..23

fear..24

follow 25

freely..26

fulfilled...27

fulfilment..28

gifts...29

gladness..30

glory...31

go 32

grace 33

guidance 34

heart...35

heartbeat 36

honour 37

hope..38

humility 39

illuminate 40

journey 41

joy 42

justice 43

king 44

kingdom 45

knowledge 46

labour 47

liberator 48

life 49

light 50

love 51

mend 52

new 53

nurture 54

nurtured 55

obedience 56

peace 57

perfection 58

pilgrim 59

pilgrimage 60

portion 61

possession 62

promise 63

protection 64

protector 65

questions 66

redeeming 67

reflection 68

reign 69

rejoice 70

remember 71

renew 72

renewal 73

riches 74

richness 75

risen 76

safe 77

salvation 78

search 79

searching 80

servant 81

shepherd 82

song 83

sovereign..84

spirit...85

spotless...86

strength..87

stronghold..88

thankful..89

transformation...90

trinity...91

trust..92

truth...93

unending..94

unity...95

universal...96

vision..97

walk..98

whole..99

wholeness...100

witness..101

worthy...102

FOREWORD

I commend these lovely verses to you. They have been written by Elizabeth Sharman-Smith and they contain many comforting words and images. The second century martyr St. Justin tells us that the seed of God's wisdom is planted in every human heart. I feel sure that Elizabeth's work contained in these pages will support many as they search for clarity, truth and meaning, which we believe can only be found in Jesus Christ. May the Lord bless all those who ponder these words and appreciate their beauty. May he move all those who unconsciously yearn for a relationship with Jesus, and may the sparks of his love, already in their hearts, be inflamed by the power of the Holy Spirit. May every experience of love draw the beloved and the lover closer to the Sacred Heart of Jesus.

Rev Canon Paul Townsend,
Ecumenical Canon, Winchester Cathedral,
(formerly Parish Priest, St. Peter's RC Church, Winchester)

adoration

May the adoration of the magi

Be a witness to you,

And prepare you

To welcome the Christ Child

Into your hearts.

And may you be filled

With the wonder of His grace.

belonging

May the look on your face

Mirror your life's story.

May your home

Be a place of peace.

May you always love God,

May you delight in His will

And may your memories

Be a delight.

beloved

Go with love in your heart

For Christ.

And with peace in your heart

For the world.

And may Almighty God

Bless you and keep you.

May you know

How blessed you are

In the name of Jesus.

blessed

May Christ's love enfold you
And may you be rich in His love.
May your smile warm the hearts
Of the lonely.
And may you always be blessed.

blessedness

May your journey be long,

And may your burden

Never overpower you.

May your heart be always willing,

And may your trust be in Christ.

May your life be fulfilled,

And may you always be loved.

blessing

May love stand proud

On the altar of your heart.

And may peace be

The guardian of your soul.

blessings

May Almighty God bless you.

May love's gift fashion you

And keep you.

May you have good health

And a long and happy life.

May you feel blessed

And may you always

Be a blessing to others.

For Jesus' sake.

CARE

May the grace of the Lord

Be upon you,

And may He keep you

In His sight,

This day and for evermore.

change

May the love of Christ

Transform you and overflow

From your heart into your life.

May you see change,

And may that change begin

In you.

changeless

May Christ's unchanging love
Gather you together
And unite you to Himself:
That all the saints in Heaven
And on the Earth,
May be made one in Him
And with Him,
Worshipping Him
For ever and ever.

Christ child

May the glory of the Christ child
Be with you today.
May peace reign in your heart
And may you know what love is,
This day and always.

consolation

May the ever open

Heart of Jesus

Console you

And remind you of

His love for you.

And may His love supply

All your needs.

constant

May your trust in

The Eternal One

Remain constant.

May you always know

That you are loved.

And may you always

Show love to others.

For Jesus' sake.

dominion

May the Lord

Strong and Mighty

Be with you today.

May He encourage you

To be confident

In all that you do.

As you follow Him

On the road leading to

His glorious dominion.

empower

May the love of Christ

Go with you and strengthen you

For the journey.

May His Spirit empower you

To be the person that you were

Meant to be.

This day and always.

enrichment

May Christ bless you.

And in the fullness

Of His love

May you be a blessing

To others.

eternity

May the Holy Spirit

Guide you on your journey

To that holy place.

May He watch over you

And keep you

In His guiding love

For eternity.

ever-loving

May Christ the ever-loving

Prince of Peace

Protect you and

Guide you through adversity.

May He exchange your darkness

For His light.

And may His holy light

Lead you to eternity.

everlasting

May Christ the everlasting

Prince of Peace

Purge your heart and mind

And renew your spirit.

May He bless you

And keep you,

And make you whole.

Faith

Go in the love of Christ.

And may God bless you

And keep you.

May His love be alive

In your heart,

To the honour and glory

Of His name.

faithful

May you encounter Christ today,

May your heart be open

To fulfil His purpose.

And in the awareness of His love

May you grow in His love,

For His sake.

fear

May you be not afraid.

May you know perfect love:

The love which casts out all fear.

And may your trust be in

God's promise:

"I will never leave you."

follow

Christ to go on before you,

Christ to enable you

And have faith in you.

Christ to comfort you,

Christ to love you

And adore you.

Freely

May your pilgrimage

To Christ and with Christ

Be continuous.

May you give freely

That which you are given freely.

And may the joy of the Lord

Always be yours.

fulfilled

May you never be lonely,

May you always have a friend.

May your life be never empty,

May your cup be ever full.

May life's wheel spin slowly for you,

And may you never want for time.

fulfilment

Go with the love of Christ

In your heart,

And with the peace of Christ

In your soul.

And may God bless you and keep you.

May His love be sufficient for you,

This day and for evermore.

gifts

May the love of Christ

Be with you today.

And may the body of Christ

Renew you today.

May the Spirit of Christ

Change you today,

And give you peace.

gladness

May the Spirit of Truth

Enter your being

And quicken you.

May the Spirit of Joy

Enter your soul

And make you glad.

glory

May the glory of the Risen Lord

Be upon you.

May you be filled with His love

And the courage to serve Him

In spirit and in truth.

To the glory of His name.

go

Go, carrying the light of Christ:

The truest and holiest

Light of all light,

Which scatters away

The dark places of the Earth.

And may God bless you

And keep you for Himself.

This day and for eternity.

GRACE

May you find your life's dream,

And may your heart be always full.

May your life overflow with charity,

And may your days be filled with grace.

May love be your protector,

And may you always love Him.

guidance

May the voice of silence

Purge your heart and mind,

And may love's mystery

Fashion your life.

May you be faithful

To your calling.

And may Christ's love

Point you to eternity.

heart

May you know how much

You are forgiven,

May you want so much

To forgive.

May love's journey

Prove eternal

And may your life

Be proved with love.

heartbeat

May the rhythm

Of your heartbeat

Inspire your soul

To make beautiful music

For God.

honour

Go in the love of Christ.

And may the peace of Christ

Be with you

And stay with you,

All the days of your life.

To the honour and glory of

His name.

hope

May your prayers be answered

And may all that you hope for

Come to fruition.

May life be kind to you.

And may you always

Bring glory to God.

humility

May humility

Be your garment.

May the glory of

The risen Christ

Shine brightly upon you,

And make you whole.

illuminate

May the glorious light of Christ

Illuminate your presence.

May love conquer your heart,

And may your actions

Be always worthy of your soul.

journey

May your journey be long
And may life's mysteries
Be opened up before you.
May the wisdom and
Boundless love of Christ
Profoundly influence you,
And make you whole.

joy

Go with love in your heart

For Christ,

With peace in your heart

For the world,

And with a joyful spirit.

And may Almighty God

Bless you and keep you.

May Christ's light

Shine brightly upon you,

This day and for evermore.

justice

May the ever open heart

Of Jesus

Heal your wounds,

And restore your soul

From all injustice

And brokenness.

May the ever-loving

Prince of Peace

Guide you

And make you whole.

king

May the King of Love

Honour you with His grace,

Secure you with his word,

And transform you with His love.

For His name's sake.

kingdom

May the inextinguishable

Love of Christ

Strengthen you

For the journey,

And may life's challenges

Produce fruit

Fit for the Kingdom.

For Jesus' sake.

knowledge

Go in the knowledge

And the love of Christ,

Knowing that He

Has truly forgiven you

And that He will keep

His promise to you

For ever.

labour

May your day be long and fruitful

And may your heart be filled with love.

May your work never overpower you

And may your labour always be light.

May your home be always welcoming

And may your family be blessed.

liberator

May Christ, both captor

And liberator of your soul,

Grant you a deeper understanding

Of His will;

That through His love for you

You may enjoy the freedom

Of His mercy

And the wonder

Of His grace.

life

May you find your life's purpose

And may it be your living art.

May your life be a journey

That will have no end.

And may the garden of your soul

Grow like swathes of incense

Offering up prayers to the Almighty.

light

May Christ's light be with you

As you walk along the way.

May your speech settle like the dew

That falls gently on the meadow.

And like the young deer

Who treads soft-footed on the grass,

May your countenance

Be a blessing to others.

May your love for your neighbour

Fulfil all that you hope for in a friend.

And may your life be filled

With longing for that day

When all shall be revealed.

love

Go in the love of Christ.

And may you be aware of

Every blessing given to you,

To do His work in the world.

And may the grace of Him

Whose name is Love

Keep you in His love,

For His sake.

mend

May the wholeness of Christ

Mend your brokenness,

And may your soul

Find its rest

In Him.

new

May the blood of Christ

Wash you.

May the word of Christ

Feed you.

And may the glory of

The risen Christ

Inspire you.

This day and for evermore.

NURTURE

May God the Father,

God the Son,

And God the Holy Spirit,

Bless you and keep you.

May His love be sufficient

For you.

This night and always.

nurtured

May your soul

Be nurtured today.

And may love's promise

Keep you in all goodness,

For His sake.

obedience

May your heart be obedient

To do Christ's will in the world.

May your love be strong enough

For the journey.

And may Almighty God bless you

And keep you for Himself,

This day and always.

peace

Go with love in your heart

For Christ,

And with peace in your heart

For mankind.

And may Almighty God

Bless you and keep you

All the days of your life,

And for eternity.

perfection

May the window

Of your soul

Be transparent,

And may perfect love

Exude from your heart.

pilgrim

May the Almighty God

Bless you and keep you.

May He guide you

On your Journey

To that holy and eternal place:

Where suffering

Will be forgotten.

pilgrimage

May the Holy Spirit

Of Truth and Love,

Strengthen you

For the journey

And renew your spirit.

May He watch over you

On your pilgrimage

To that heavenly country:

Where your soul will find

What it truly longs for.

portion

May the passage of time

Never weary you.

May peace be your companion

And may love be your portion.

For Jesus' sake.

possession

May you find

What possesses you.

And with the gift of time

May you possess it.

promise

May your love move mountains
In the coldest of hearts.
May your eye fall upon goodness,
And may your smile show
The goodness of your own heart.
May the song of your heart
Weave its way through channels
Of broken dreams
And mend them.
And when life gets bitter
May Love's promise
Be revealed to you.

pROTECTION

May the light of Christ

Direct you in all that you do.

And may the love of Christ

Protect you and console you

In all your ways.

This day and for always.

pROTECTOR

May the God of truth and love

Who draws you to Himself

Keep you for Himself,

This night

And for evermore.

questions

May the peace of the Lord

Go with you.

May life be kind to you.

May you find answers

To your questions.

And may your dreams

Be fulfilled.

Redeeming

May the redeeming Blood

Of Jesus

Protect you in all adversity.

And may the Spirit

Of Jesus

Perfect you in all your ways.

Reflection

May God's love be with you.

May the prism of His light

Shine brightly upon you

And reflect His holiness,

From the beginning

Of each and every day

Until its end.

Reign

May the Lord be with you.

May peace reign

In your heart,

And may you bring

Honour and glory

To the Prince of Peace.

This day and for evermore.

Rejoice

May you live your life to the full.

And may you have the eye to see

Every blessing granted to you,

And every heart that the Creator

Has entrusted to you.

May you be for ever thankful.

And may your spirit for ever rejoice.

Remember

Go and remember

That Jesus chooses

Not to see who you were,

But who you are now.

And may Almighty God bless you

And keep you for Himself,

This day, and for evermore.

Renew

May Christ who makes all things new

Write His word upon your heart.

May He deliver you

In days of trouble,

And grant you peace in your time.

For the honour and glory of His name.

Renewal

May Christ, the maker

Of all that is good,

Renew your hearts and minds.

May His everlasting arms

Reach out to save you.

And may you be willing to change,

For His sake.

Riches

May the finger of opportunity

Point at you,

Touch you, and make you glad.

May your riches serve you

And may your life be made richer

By the poor.

richness

Blessed are you in Jesus' love,

Blessed are you

When you know how much

He cares for you.

May His love protect you

And keep you,

As you journey on.

And may your life be made richer

For His sake.

Risen

May the Spirit of the risen Christ

Comfort you and draw you closer

To Himself.

May the body and blood

Of Our Lord Jesus Christ

Cleanse you from all unrighteousness

And make you whole.

And may the blessing of

God the Father,

God the Son,

And God the Holy Spirit,

Be with you for evermore.

safe

May you let Christ

Carry your burden, today,

As you follow Him

Along the path of the narrow way

That will keep you from wrongdoing.

May His love keep you safe.

And may His grace

Be sufficient for you.

salvation

May the God of your salvation

Summon you to His courts,

And may you find there

Peace and justice

For your soul.

search

May the longing

Of your heart's whisper

Draw you closer

To Him who called you.

May you find your

Innermost centre,

That pearl of great price.

May you live with it for ever,

And may it give you peace.

searching

May your heart be untroubled.

May you find

What you are looking for.

And may what you are looking for

Bring you peace.

servant

Go in the name of Jesus.

And may the blood of Jesus

Cleanse you,

May the body of Jesus

Serve you,

And may the Spirit of Jesus

Direct you in all goodness;

For His love's sake.

shepherd

May that great shepherd

Of the sheep

Guide you along the narrow way

To pastures new.

And may His love supply

All your needs.

Now, and always.

song

May the song on your lips

Bear witness to the love in your heart.

May you always care for goodness,

And may you never be put to shame.

May you be for ever thankful,

And may all your memories be good.

sovereign

May the joy of the Risen Lord
Be always with you.
And may His peace
Reign in your heart,
Now and for evermore.

spirit

May beauty enter your soul,

And may you receive

The gift of forgiveness.

May compassion

Be your garment,

And may you know

That you are truly loved.

spotless

May Christ, who makes

All things new,

Write his word upon your heart:

That you may stand spotless

In His sight for evermore.

STRENGTH

May The Lord Jesus Christ

Bless you

And keep you for Himself.

May you grow in His grace,

And may the overpowering

Strength of His love

Carry you to everlasting life.

stronghold

May Jesus Christ,

The everlasting stronghold,

Keep your heart and mind

In the Father's love.

May you seek his truth always.

And may your heart be ever open

To do His will.

thankful

Go with a thankful heart.
And remember
Every blessing that God
Has bestowed upon you,
Each joy that the creator
Has blessed you with,
And each heart that
He has entrusted to you.
For His love's sake.

Transformation

May the glory of the risen Christ

Transform your ordinary life

Into an extraordinary work for God.

And through His love shown to others,

By your forgiveness of them,

May you find everlasting peace.

In Jesus' name.

trinity

May God the Father of all

Look kindly upon you;

May Christ the Son of God

Bless you;

And may His Holy Spirit

Guide you and keep you

For His purpose,

This day and for evermore.

TRUST

May you let Christ
Carry your burden today.
May His love enfold you,
And may His spirit
Draw you closer
To Himself.

truth

May the God of all truth

And love

Surround you with

Every blessing

To do His will.

And may He give you

Everlasting peace.

unending

Go with a peaceful heart.

And may the risen Christ

Bless you and keep you.

May you know

The wonder of His grace,

This day and for evermore.

unity

May the unchangeable love

Of Jesus

Unite you to Himself,

That you may be made

One spirit with Him,

Worshipping Him

For ever and ever.

universal

May the creator of the universe

Bind you together

With His love,

Transform you

With his ever-loving grace,

And fill your longing heart

With thanksgiving.

For the honour and glory

Of His name.

vision

May the unconditional

Love of Jesus,

Transform your brokenness.

May the vision of the risen Lord

Inspire you,

And make you whole.

walk

May your walk be with Christ.

May love's promise guide you

On your journey.

May your heart be a home

That welcomes the stranger.

And may love's heartbeat

Find its way through

Distant memories,

And heal you.

whole

May the mighty love of Jesus

Strengthen you.

May the anointing Spirit of Jesus

Comfort you.

And may the miraculous life of Jesus

Be an example to you,

And make you whole.

wholeness

May the healing Love

Of Christ

Enter your being.

And in the fullness

Of time

Make you whole.

witness

May Christ's healing love

Anoint you.

May His Holy and comforting Spirit

Guide you.

And may His sacrificial blood

Cleanse you and empower you to be

A witness to Him in the world.

And may the blessing of God,

The Father, God the Son

And God the Holy Spirit,

Be with you this day

And for evermore.

worthy

May the glorious light

Of Christ

Illuminate your journey.

May His transforming love

Conquer your heart.

And may your actions

For ever reflect

His love for you.